INVESTING IN A TINY HOUSE

PETRU VANTU

INTRODUCTION

As at 2013, an average single-family house was 2,598 s□uare feet. That is according to the United States Census Bureau. All these units have a variety of accessories from air conditioning, stories, basements, forced - air furnaces, bathrooms, etcetera. Needless to say, this large living ultimately results in lots of overheads. Apart from the expenses involved in building and maintaining these superfluous units, there is also too much usage of electricity and gas. The tiny house movement solves these challenges and more.

Living small is living green. If you are living in less s□uare feet, your energy needs will automatically go down. Over half a million air conditioning units are needed to sustain the 2,598 s□uare units of houses. Reduce the square footage per house and the air conditioners that are needed will drastically reduce which will have a positive impact on the utility bills. Tiny houses have a smaller carbon footprint which is what we need to be vouching for if we intend to save this planet from the looming decline.

Most city dwellers are crippled by huge debts thanks to the mortgages they have on their homes. A house that would typically cost $290,000 if paid for in a single payment will eventually cost over a million if paid out using the hire purchase model that mortgages are based on. Most people spend their entire lifetime trying to clear mortgages and some even lose their houses when for one reason or another they are unable to continue with the monthly payments. The solution to this is living in tiny houses. It is cheaper and sustainable.

Even though we all naturally love more space, green living is a concept that is catching on with remarkable speed thanks to the tiny house movement. More people are subscribing to the sustainable lifestyle school of thought. That would explain why the topic is increasingly becoming popular not only on social media but also on mainstream media like CNN, Guardian, AP, NPC, etcetera.

Not everybody might find it necessary to make such a drastic change in their lives in the name of sustainable living. However, any revolution that left a huge mark on earth was never led by masses. That is why the tiny house movement has a great chance of shaping the future of mankind. Tiny house communities might soon be common place across the continents of the world but especially so in the industrialized countries. Green living is what mother earth needs to keep alive.

Want To Simplify Your Life?

Want To Lower Your Monthly Expenses?

Want To Reduce Your Dependency On Your Job?

Tiny Houses May Be The Answer For You And Your Family.

THANKS AGAIN FOR DOWNLOADING THIS BOOK,

I'M SURE YOU'LL ENJOY READING IT!

INTRODUCTION

CHAPTER ONE

INTRODUCTION TO TINY HOUSE MOVEMENT

What Is A Tiny House Movement?

People are talking about the tiny house movement. What is it? Is it small houses that are being moved down the street to tiny lots? Is it a political moveme nt? This moveme nt is all about a segment of society that states that people are downsizi ng the space or spaces that they live in.

If you haven't heard of it, the tiny house movement is a growing trend and not just a fad. It's been featured on network television all over the world. What makes the tiny movement so big and what determines what a small home is? The average house in America is just less than 3,000 s□uare feet in size. Tiny houses are built with the focus on smaller simplified living so they average around 400 to 500 s□uare feet at the most. Some small houses are very tiny, at around 65 s□uare feet.

When Did Tiny Houses Begin Blooming?

Turns out to be that during the Katrina Hurricane disaster in 2005, Marianne Cusato developed 308 sq. ft. cottage constructions for the homeless victims and the small house movements bloomed.

Can You Get What You Want in Your Small Home Plan?

If you have to give up the things you want in a home just for the speed, you've made the wrong choice. Small homes and speedy build times are great goals but you'll want to be sure you get what you want.

To be sure you do, prioritize your list of wants and convey this to your home's designer. Take your time before you begin building and before you get any loan. Preparation is critical. Knowing what you want is the key factor. You will likely have to make compromises but with patient preparation, those compromises won't result in losing things you truly want.

How Did The Tiny-House Movement Start?

Multiple factors fueled the growth of the miniature-house movement. As thousands of people lost their homes due to unemployment or foreclosure during the 2007–08 financial crisis, many turned to tiny homes as an affordable alternative to traditional housing.

Those looking to shrink their carbon footprint also found these cozy

□uarters to be energy-efficient, saving them a bundle of utilities. Others, hoping to streamline their lives, were lured by the prospect of shedding most of their belongings and living simply.

While it might have originally seemed like a passing fad, the tiny-home trend is actually growing. While the exact number of tiny homes is unknown, in 2015 alone more than 30 microcommunities—established or under development—sprouted up across the U.S., according to Tiny House Community, a website for owners.

But Why The Movement Toward Downsizing Houses?

This movement is all about efficiency, saving natural resources, and saving the environment. People who have been concerned about these factors in society have been very concerned at a number of natural resources (and accompanying waste) that are generated every time a standard size home is built.

And if you include all the resources that go into maintaining older standard size houses, a good argument can be made that the old adage of "Bigger is better" is not better anymore. For example: If a tiny home of about 200 s□uare feet is built in remote areas away from sprawling cities, the house leaves virtually no impact or carbon footprint on the natural environment around it. And in many areas, small houses are using solar panels for their energy source.

Super Reasons To Quit (Or Down-Size) The Mortgage:

Unfortunately, life doesn't always work out in line with our plans. For many, our incomes and financial situations fall short of satisfying the hopes and dreams of our very own cozy nook. Some have very few options due to a low income or a high debt level and the relative lack of informed choices targeted to our budget level.

It hardly seems fair - isn't everyone entitled to the Great American Dream?

Small Houses are solution for those who have grown despairing of crippling mortgages. They're also a hugely reduced mortgage alternative for a first time home buyer - especially when coupled with first time home buyer programs or grants. With the advent of a new and growing trend leaning towards small houses and plans for small inexpensive house designs, people of any means can now have the home that they desire and deserve.

Mortgages have been stock-standard practice for decades when it comes to home ownership. Now you can build your own smaller-sized home with plans for small inexpensive house designs. From small house plans and unusual small homes to tiny houses and micro homes - there are small and tiny house plans and designs to suit everyone's taste. Minimizing the space in which you live allows you many freedoms from mortgage worries.

1. **Income From A Job Is Not Guaranteed:**

We can see that clearly with lay-offs and redundancies in the current depressed economy. Having no more mortgage or a smaller mortgage limits your exposure to crippling debt levels if your income temporarily takes a dive.

2. **The Interest Rates That You Agree To At the Time You Purchase Your House Multiply Anytime The Banks Want To Increase Them.**

This e□uals uncertain and out-of-your-control repayments for homeowners. With no mortgage, you can watch the news reports of rate rises and know that you're immune to all of that worry now. While you'll still experience a rise in your repayments with a small house loan, comparatively you'll be paying out less than a rise in a larger mortgage.

3. **When Adults Need To Work Full-Time, Have Multiple Jobs And Take on Some Overtime To Keep The House, Family**

Time Is Limited:

Small houses give you the flexibility to invest more into your family while still managing to keep the bank happy.

4. **If Your Lifetime Is On Average 60-80 Years**, and you spend

20 years as a child, 30 years, at least, and working to pay off your loan, that only leaves you 10-30 years to enjoy your life debt free.

Hey - that's not fair or fun. Ensuring your retirement is enjoyable and arrives a lot sooner is a solid and compelling reason to go small or tiny with your house and loan.

5. **Financial Strain Causes Relationships To Fracture, Or Even Disintegrate Entirely.**

Changing to smaller house and debt levels can change your relationship in a way that you never imagined a bank could be a part of!

6. **Need A Holiday Once Or Twice A Year?**
   I'm afraid that might need to wait a little while longer as you still need to pay down the debt. Smaller homes shorten the timespan of the loan and reduce your payments giving you more holiday and relaxation time. That's reason enough all by itself for anyone to downsize their home and mortgage!

7. **It Happens All The Time - chronic health problems can disable a family's income earning potential.** A spate of bad health in your family may mean you need to stay home as a caregiver but the bank still needs their money. No choice but to work and pay up or you're out! Go small or tiny and your family's health takes the front seat to a greater degree.

8. **The Savings In Monthly Expenses Alone Are Enough To Make You Want To Start Building Your Own Small House.**Smaller house plans take a large step towards reducing the cost of your monthly utility bills.

Imagine your electricity bill between $30 and $60 every month. You could even use solar panels or a wind turbine to eliminate the need to pay the bill at all - better still, make money from the electric company when you sell them power.

Right now, the average cost of an established house in America is $250,000. Then you add in all of your expenses - house payments, bills, utilities, property taxes, fees and regulations over the life of a mortgage... there's not a lot left at the end of the month. Your home should enhance your lifestyle not make you want to run from it!

Downsizing to Simple Housing Is the Answer for Some

There are some people who have not been affected by natural disasters or financial meltdowns. They simply want to join the movement because, for a lot of people in today's hectic society, simplicity is king.

Many people in society during the last few decades have found themselves working long work weeks and getting little time off, only to spend that time constantly maintaining a large house that they hardly ever spent any time in. Although small homes will always be just that, the tiny house movement is growing into something big.

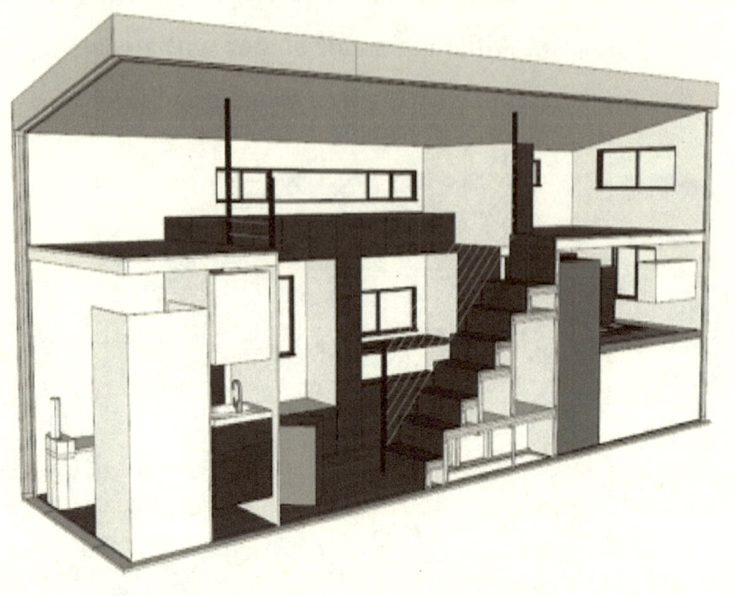

Where To Find Small House Plans

If you are interested in small house plans you should always look for the best deals on blueprints. Blueprints or plans are available from a variety of sources and at many different prices. Two of my favorites are coolhouseplans.com and dongardner.com. Plans from cool house plans have prices ranging from $585 for five sets of blueprints up to $1,175 for CAD files. If you are not familiar with CAD files, these are Computer Aided Drawing files, meaning that they provide all the information needed to build the house on CD-ROM and have blueprints that can be printed and as often as needed and in any □uantity.

Materials for these homes are usually lower in cost since they don't re□uire as much wood or brick. Someone interested in small house plans can also look for designer who can make custom blueprints with all the specific features you want. These custom plans may cost less than complete house blueprints or they may cost more - depending on the designer or architect. You can also find kits that come with plans where the home can be built in a few weeks or months.

Myths About Tiny House Living

Over the years, there have been myths and misconceptions about tiny house living on meida and other reality shows. In order to set the record straight by debunking 10 tiny house myths.

1. Tiny House Living Is Easy.

This is the most popular myth. Tiny house living is not easy. Yes, there are aspects of the life that are easier– less stuff equals less cleaning but living in a tiny house won't solve all your problems. Tiny houses and Airstreams have problems of their own too! While living in Airstream you had to fix both the hot water heater and the air conditioner. Not easy or cheap! But not as cost as bigger house

You can build or buy a tiny house for cheaper and the energy savings/lifestyle savings will add up over time, but do not be fooled into thinking that tiny house living is a quick money saving trick.

2. Tiny House Living Is Glamorous.

Living in tiny can be glamorous but it requires lot of work and commitment to cleaning the little space you got. Tiny house can be messy a lot considering the little space. Don't be caught unaware. To be fair, Tiny house requires 75% of your time for cleaning anf putting everything in good shape.

3. There's No Privacy.

There is privacy in a tiny home if you plan for it and if you respect other people's boundaries. I've seen tiny houses where the loft is closed off for privacy. I've also seen a lot of sliding doors or pocket doors. Therefore, you can easily enjoy your privacy with a proper planning

4. You Can't Have A Big Family, More Than One Pet, Etc.

Living in a tiny house is a matter of what you learn to tolerate. And some people won't be able to adapt. Its harsh, but it's true. If you have four dogs or four kids, can you adapt to being physically close to them 24/7? If you can't, tiny house living is not for you. If you can learn to be around your loved ones (furry and not so furry) all the time, then you can do it.

5. You Have To Be Naturally Handy.

We live in a wonderful age. An age where you can look up almost anything online and there will be a video or instructions or a forum on how to do it. (Airforum is great for Airstream tips and tricks, Tiny House Community is great for tiny houses.)

6. You Have To Travel With Your Tiny Home.

For some people traveling in their tiny home is not possible. For whatever reason, they are tied to a place.

7. Tiny Homes Must Be Built On A Trailer Bed Or Less Than 200 Square Feet Or Diyed!

People get an idea in their head that tiny houses must have a bunch of rigid standards. Tiny houses have to be less than 200 s□uare feet! Tiny houses have to be built on a trailer bed! Tiny houses have to be DIYed! Well, none of that is true. Tiny house living is about living a smaller space, but also about living a more meaningful life.

8. You Have To Give Up Everything.

Living tiny is all about prioritizing. You don't have to give up your entire world, hobbies, collections and loved ones to live in a tiny house, but you do have to set some strict priorities. Pick one or two hobbies that are important to you and leave space for those things. It's going to be very hard if you have a large library, you like to can vegetables, you are a crafter and your loved one is a carpenter with a penchant for motorcycles. Pick one or two hobbies that you truly love and run with them. You don't have to give up everything.

9. You Don’t Have To Give Up Anything!

That being said, you do have to give up some things. And you must have harsh parameters. It’s unrealistic to think that you can have all the hobbies and toys and the same life you had living in a large house. Be ready to loose some of your belongings.

The Advantages Of Living In Tiny Houses

Below are list of the many benefits of owning a tiny home. Here we go...

1. **Less Initial Cost**

A tiny house is obviously smaller than a traditional home. There are fewer materials and the labor re□uired to build it because of its size. Since tiny homes often have most of the features a traditional house has (kitchen, plumbing, roof, flooring) the price per square foot is usually more expensive. But since overall size of the house is so much smaller, the overall price is only a fraction of traditional homes.

2. Less Energy Consumption

Tiny homes re□uire much less energy to heat and cool simply because they have much less interior air space. Since many tiny homes are on wheels, a tiny house owner could move their house under a large tree in the summer, and out into the sun during the winter. Two additional culprit's for significant energy consumption are refrigerators and hot water heaters. Both are typically smaller in a tiny house and consume far less energy. Another use of energy is your own energy. It doesn't take long to tidy up a very small dwelling. I have seen folks who have been very creative with reducing their tiny house's energy consumption and making use of the fact that their home is very small. Solar panels, wood stoves, wind turbines, compost toilets, the list goes on and on.

3. Less Water Consumption And Trash

If you have a small shower and small hot water heater, chances are your showers will be a lot shorter. If you have a small trash can, chances are you will generate less trash. Using less water and producing less trash is both good for the environment and your wallet.

4. Less Cost For Repairs

Repair costs for your tiny home are simply a matter of mathematics. The cost to replace the roof of a 2,000 s□uare foot home will be a lot less than the cost of a 300 s□uare foot home. This is of course because of the reduction in materials and labor.

5. **Less Land To Purchase And Upkeep**

A small dwelling will re□uire less land resides on. Since many cities have restrictions on the size a home can be, you may be re□uired to purchase land outside the city with no restrictions. Land outside the city is cheaper to purchase and the taxes are less. If you elect to buy a very small plot of land that your house will reside on, you'll spend less time cutting grass. If you buy a regular sized lot, you'll have more room your garden.

6. **Less Food**

If you have a small pantry, you'll have a small amount of food in your house. If you can look through your kitchen window and see fresh vegetables growing in it, you'll spend less produce. By eating less food in your tiny house, you'll keep your food bill and weight down.

7. **Less Taxes**

Since the value of your tiny home and land is resides on is less valuable (assuming you choose to buy your land rather than lease) your tax bill will be less. The savings can go towards investments, retirement, college for your children, vacations, or donations to tinyhouselistings.com:-)

8. **Less Insurance**

Insurance for your home can add up uickly, especially when it comes time to use it. Tiny houses cost much less to insure because they are less valuable. Many insurance companies consider tiny houses on wheels to be an RV. Since insurance companies aren't nonprofits and are in business to make money, you will often have difficulty getting the money from them. By owning a tiny house you can minimize the amount you give to them in the first place.

9. Less Interest Paid

When I bought my first house, initially I was paying more towards interest than the principle. It's no secret that over the course of a 30-year loan, you will pay more for interest than you will the house itself. Most tiny house owners elect to pay cash for their tiny house or to pay it off quickly. The amount you save by avoiding interest will ultimately be a huge amount. More than enough to buy the in-laws a tiny house and have it located on the back (way back) of your property.

10. More Disposable Income

All of the above reasons I've listed for buying a tiny house have been focused on "less". Less consumption, less money out of pocket. All of this leads to having more money in the bank at your disposal. If you write a list of your recurring expenses, you'll uickly realize that costs associated with your home represent the majority of your expenses. By owning and living in a tiny house, you are slashing your living expenses at every level.

11. More Freedom

Ok, 11 reasons. I saved the best for last. When you own and live in a small house, you free up your two most precious resources, money and time, not to mention some of Earth's most precious resources...water and energy.

Does your current standard of living prevents you from working at the job you want?

Does it prevent you from going on vacations and taking time off when you like?

Do you have to sacrifice spending time doing exactly what you want simply to pay your bills?

Are you worried about the Earth and environment and leaving it in good shape for those that follow us? By living in a tiny house, you free up money by cutting expenses in a big way. You use less natural resources. You free up time by spending less on it cleaning and maintaining your home. You trade s□uare feet for freedom.

12. Aids Environment Protection

Unarguably, the biggest appeal that small houses carry for buyers, is that they are environment-friendly. For people concerned with environmental degradation, this is the major drawing factor and with good reason. Micro houses not only take up less space but also prevent the uprooting of trees.

13. Promotes Clutter-Free Living

One unintended benefit that a small house entails, is promoting a clutter-free lifestyle amongst the inhabitants. Since there is a lack of space, the inhabitants have to make tough choices with regard to what they want to keep and what they want to discard. This helps in ensuring that the occupant's live a cleaner and more organized life.

Tiny House Cost Vs Traditional House Cost

According to CBS News, the average cost of a home in the United States is $156,100. The below numbers show the average price of a home, the interest paid and the total of both the home cost and the interest paid. The numbers also show the same for a tiny dwelling. Although I don't have statistics on the average price of a tiny house, based on my observation I would say the median price is somewhere around $25,000. Some cost less and some that come with all of the bells and whistles cost more.

The numbers also show the interest paid on a 30-year note for a traditional house and a 15-year note for a tiny house at 4.5% interest.

How Much Can Be Saved By Purchasing A Tiny Home?

Cost of the house

Traditional house = $156,100

Tiny house = $25,00

Interest Paid

Traditional house (30 year loan) = $128,636.87

Tiny house (15 year loan) = $9,424.70

Total Paid (cost + interest)

Traditional house = $284.736.87

Tiny House = $34,424.70

This means that the cost of a tiny home only represents approximately 12% of the cost of an average traditional home.

Don't Be A Slave To Your Big House, Demerits Of A Bigger House

The best thing about having a bigger home is that you will have more space. You will have more rooms which can be used in a variety of ways. Rooms can be specifically designated as study areas, libraries, music room, gym or whatever you desire. More rooms mean that you can have guest bedrooms for family and friends to stay, and a bedroom for each of the kids. Everyone will get their own space.

But considering the hidden cost and other disadvantages that come with big house fully understand the implications of what owning a larger home meant.

1. **A Bigger Home, Bigger Utility Bills.**

When calculating our monthly budget costs, we, of course, factored in the larger mortgage payment. What we didn't do was calculate how much the additional space would mean to our electric, gas and other utility bills. It's easy to forget that additional bathrooms mean additional water, or that more bedrooms mean added TVs, lights and cable boxes, all of which drive up electric and cable costs respectively.

2. **You'll Need Additional Help To Maintain It:**

If you are working full-time, or even if you're not, keeping a large home clean takes a lot of work. While my husband and I made a concerted effort to keep the house straightened and clean, with three children we just couldn't keep up. We finally relented and got some help every two weeks. While it made a huge difference in our time and our stress levels, it was another item we had neglected to budget in our initial finances.

3. **Landscaping And Property Maintenance Costs Are Larger:**

We were advised by a landscape designer that people always underestimate the cost of landscaping when building a new home. Their rule of thumb was to allocate 10 percent of the cost of the house to the purchase of trees, shrubs, and plants. Needless to say, we didn't include the price of all the foundation plantings, side barriers etc, in the cost of our house.

Our other realization over time, all those foundation plantings need to be cut back and trimmed each year once they reach maturity. And unless you plan on spending a few hours every weekend maintaining the lawn, add in lawn care maintenance for mowing and fertilizing each year.

4. **Additional Space Means More Rooms To Furnish.**

When we first moved into our new home, we had enough furniture to fill a bedroom, nursery, and a small living room. Calls placed to our home sounded like they were taking place in an empty airplane hanger. The costs of decorating and furnishing extra rooms can be quite expensive, re□uiring furniture, window treatments, rugs, lamps, paintings, etc. While we convinced ourselves that this was an expense we could pay out over time, the echoing rooms got old very fast.

5. **The Imbalance Is Energetic:**

A house is inanimate, or in human terms dead. The furniture, clothing, artwork, carpet, and mechanical systems of a house are also inanimate. We are animate, or alive, and equally important, we are social animals. When we are in a setting in which there are more dead things than live things, as in the too big house, we lose energy to the house... When we are in a setting in which there are more dead things than live things, as in the too big house, we lose energy to the house. We can feel its emptiness, a loneliness, a sense that something is missing, and often compensate for that by animating it with things that make us feel good. The effect of the adding inanimate things is to feel an initial enchantment making us feel we are getting energy, e.g., the happiness one feels at the addition of a beautiful new table. However, that excitement dissipates rather quickly, and we are left with another energy deficit.

6. **Relationship Dangers**

Aside from feeling an emptiness and a lack of containment from being in a too large house, there are serious negative consequences for an intimate relationship. Unless such a home is used regularly to entertain or otherwise host large numbers of people, the deadness and the vastness of the space becomes metaphors for the state of the relationship. The house will often end up re□uiring either or both much time/money to maintain, taking time/money away from the relationship; the house comes between the couple. Energetically, as mentioned above, each person is being drained by the deadness of the house and has less energy for the partner.

Five Of the Smallest Houses in the World

1. **Tumbleweed Houses**

Since 1997, Jay Shafer of the Tumbleweed Tiny House Company has been living in houses that range from just 50 to 750 s□uare feet. Despite the tiny size, however, they still manage to fit everything he could possibly need inside - a workspace, bedroom, bathroom with toilet and shower and even a living space.

2. Micro Compact Home

They say that small things come in small packages and in this case, it might just be true. Measuring just 2.6m cubed, Micro Compact Homes somehow manage to include room for two double beds, a bathroom, lobby, dining space, kitchen and top of the range technology. We bet they have a fair few items in self-storage though because we can't imagine there is room for much else after that.

3. Rollit Homes

Students at the University of Karlsruhe in Germany used their creative skills to design a set of homes that have been built to incorporate multiple uses inside one small living space. Although it may sound bizarre, the home functions like a mouse on a wheel. The homeowner can change the structure of the house by walking in the center to rotate it. This clever idea means that with a little bit of effort, the house can be turned to reveal a bed, lounge chair, table, shower, toilet or a kitchen - all in one tiny space.

4. Quay House

As the smallest house in Great Britain, Quay House is, in fact, a tourist attraction in Wales that measures a measly 10 feet by 6 feet. Unbelievably, the last person to occupy the house was 6 foot 3 inches tall yet there was still enough space for a bed, bedside cabinet, stove and water tap.

5. **Nano House**

Created to help solve the world's global housing crisis, Nano Living System Houses are just 25 square-meters yet are designed to fit a family of four. Despite the lack of space, the homes look incredibly modern, are e□uipped with state-of-the-art insulation, have passive solar heating and the rooms are even convertible to make the most of the small space.

Five Reasons Why You Should Get Your Tiny House Washing Once Every 6 Months

1. **It Gives Your House A New Look**

When you want to infuse some new life in the exterior of your home in order to creates a better visual impact, the first thing that you can do is to soft wash your house to which will refreshen its appearance and add new value to your home. A need for power washing services is strongly indicated when the exterior of your house starts showing signs of accumulating dirt, mold and mildew, fungus and rust stains. All these undesirable elements make your house look dirty and old. When you soft wash the exterior of your home it gets a bright new look.

Although many people get their houses washed after yearly and some after four or five years it is advisable to get your house soft washed every six months to one year especially when there is more exposure to vehicular pollution and foot traffic as well.

2. **It Increases The Value Of Your House**

If you decide to sell your house at any time, you can always ensure a much better price if you get your house washed just before you put it up for sale. The washing will give your house a fresh clean look and will greatly increase its curb appeal and value.

When your house looks clean and attractive from the outside it will make someone also want to see it from the inside. If the house does not have a clean and appealing exterior it may deter a potential buyer right away without any interest in seeing the interior of your house, which may, in fact, be very beautiful.

3. **It Prevents Damage To Your Paint**

Other than washing your house to clean it up for cosmetic sprucing you need to wash your house to protect your exterior paint. The paint job on the exterior of your home is affected by the dust, grime, and also mold and mildew especially in north facing walls or those parts of the house that are shaded by trees and shrubbery and receive little or no sunlight.

Mould thrives in humid moist conditions where ventilation is poor and condensation occurs due to poor circulation of air. Mould penetrates the surface of the paint and keeps growing underneath it and can lead to deterioration and peeling of a painted surface. Even if you paint over mold, it continues to grow under it. Therefore it is essential to remove mold by soft washing using chlorine in the water.

4. **It Removes And Prevents The Growth Of Mold And Mildew**

If the weather is generally humid it is conducive for mold and mildew to grow and thrive. Even under normal weather conditions mold and mildew to grow as a natural phenomenon pursuant to changes in the weather favorable to their growth.

Therefore to be on the safer side, it is advisable to get your house washed every six months for preventing the growth of mold and mildew. Soft washing the house removes mold and regular washing every six months can prevent mold from growing on the walls, roofs, and other places.

5. **You Remain Healthier And Buy Less Medication**

Mould affects the health of people who are exposed to it. People are mainly affected by breathing in spores or tiny fragments of mold. Skin contact is also a way to be affected by mold that can happen by touching moldy surfaces or by swallowing mold. Although risks from the mould may vary from one person to another usual mold exposure leads to a cough, sore throat, nasal and sinus congestion, wheezing or other breathing difficulties, eye and skin irritation etc.

When you remove and prevent mold growth by soft washing every six months you automatically reduce your medical bills, as you will need to buy fewer medications for a cough, sinus, and asthma because you will have removed potential sources causing these ailments from the house.

Challenges Facing the Ecological Tiny House?

There are some serious problems that these houses are facing making them difficult to be a replacement for the masses.

- **One Of The Challenges Are The Legal Issue.**In most areas, there are zoning and codes that buildings must meet up to. These tiny houses are so small that they don't really fit into a proper legal category. Much of the time the law doesn't know what to do with them so many times they are just not allowed. There will have to be some acceptance of this type of lifestyle choice on the legal level for it to work out for the masses.

- **The Other Issue Is Cost.** Most of these homes are not mass produced by any means. They are built by hand with high □uality and efficient parts. This makes the cost per s□uare foot of these houses extremely high compared to other homes. For many, the idea of paying a high price for something so small puts them off when the same money could buy something that is quite a bit larger. It's hard to sell the advantages of efficiency and low impact on resources when there are larger which tends to mean better deals out there in many people's minds.

Even if the tiny house is a niche market it does show a practical example of how people could live much simpler in today's modern context. Whether this lifestyle becomes one for the masses or not, it does prove a point. At this point in time, these challenges are real and the biggest hurdle that many have to face is wanting to use a home like this.

CHAPTER TWO

TIPS ON BUYING AND SELLING TINY HOUSE

Buying Tiny Homes for Sale Vs Building Your Own

Here are a few important factors in the choice of whether to build or buy.

1. **Construction Skills**

While most people can improvise a structure in the wilderness, the bamboo-and-leaf structures of lost wouldn't be up to the building codes in most suburbs. Not only are there some basic carpentry skills and a whole set of tools that become necessary, but would-be-builders should also consider the need for more complex skills involving electrician work and plumbing. The DIY route is appealing, but the average handyman is □uickly out of his depth with this project.

2. **Specialized Materials**

The amateur contractor may have some serious remodeling projects under his or her belt, but building a structure on a trailer re□uires special considerations for weight and durability. The tiny homes for sale by professionals are built to handle travel at highway speeds when a little wobble in the wind can tor□ue the whole structure. Other residences may only experience comparable strain in an earth□uake or hurricane, but many of the people who live in 100 s□uare feels need to move the home every few years.

3. Professional Warranties

Shopping for homes for sale will allow you to choose between different warranties. The structure you build yourself doesn't have a professional guarantee that it will stand up to weather, time, and adverse circumstances. Contractors and turnkey builders have a range of options where your investment will be protected for months or years.

4. Potential for Resell

These little houses are not a popular investment for flippers because they don't tend to retain value well. Inhabited trailers have a similar problem, in that they are significantly less attractive after having been lived-in for years. That said, buyers looking for a deal will be far more likely to consider paying for a getaway residence that has been assembled by people with know-how. Your considerable DIY skills are difficult for a third party to evaluate, and so purchasers will likely assume that the wiring and other key components will need a thorough inspection.

Things To Consider When Buying Tiny House Kits

Purchasing the appropriate tiny house kits doesn't have to be a major hurdle and one has a lot of reasons why they are better off buying one. It is the more convenient and cost-effective option in building your dream lodge. However, before immediately buying the first one that comes around, it is essential that you do your research and considers all the available choice so that you will find the unit that fits your lifestyle and preferences. It is also important that you learn some important things about log cottages and their essential components such as cabin windows, doors, etc. so that you are able to weigh your options and make an informed decision.

When you choose lodging assembly sets you are going for an option that has a proven track record and a checkered history. Log cottages were the preferred building method in the past and were commonly used in Scandinavia, Russia and other parts of Eastern Europe. This home building concept was brought to America by the Scandinavian immigrants in the 17th century. Up until the early 19th century, most of the lodges were made out of hand-hewn timber and after a few years, milled logs were gradually introduced.

At present, when you are buying log sets you must have to consider many things before making your final decision. One of the major considerations when deciding on the most appropriate lodge assembly sets is your preferred log type. Majority of the log sets that are available in the market today are either machine-profiled or milled logs although there are still those that are made of logs that are handcrafted. One of the main advantages of logs that are machine-profiled is that these are more convenient and simpler to use. Because of this, the log cottage sets that use milled logs are more expensive. One can also explore other options that are available when you opt for logs that are machine-profiled and all these options have lesser workload.

One must understand that there are still other things to consider once you opt for the use of machine-profiled timber. There are different processing methods of milled timber and your choice will depend largely on the quality that you re□uire from the log material that you are going to use in building your dream cottage.

The assembly sets will also include all the essential components and accessories needed to complete the construction of your dream chalet. These include the doors, porches as well as other parts which the client's want in their cottage.

One of the most effective ways of familiarizing yourself with all the critical aspects about log cottages is by researching online. You can find useful information and leads to practical and best offers by checking the Websites of manufacturers and suppliers of log cottage assembly sets. In this way, you are able to broaden your options. Before making your final decision, it is important that you make an ocular inspection of your shortlisted choices and see for yourself how each of these choices fit your lifestyle and preference.

How to Make it Big With Tiny House Kits

With the emergence of advanced building systems and ready access to cranes and other heavy equipment, tiny cabin homes are becoming a popular choice both in the rural and suburban settings. These easy to assemble small log homes are pre-processed logs and usually come as tiny house kits. The logs are the predominant feature of the exterior as well as the interior of the tiny home structure. The log cabin kit follows a carefully developed template for an ideal rustic design complete with the re□uisite cabin windows, doors and even partitions. For most of us who want to have a log cabin for functional reasons or even as an addition to your home property must seriously consider the small cabin kit.

If you want to go through the trouble in your dealings with the architect, construction specialist, carpenter, plumber and other professionals to complete your small home construction or improvement project then buying a small cabin kit is your best alternative. Once you already made up your mind to start with the project, the first thing that you have to firm up is your budget for the project.

You have to make a list of all the essential services that you will require in completing your project. Before you start the project, finalize how you are going to finance your project. Are you going to utilize your e□uity or are you going to seek to finance for your project.

You also must meet all the State documentary requirements and other re□uisites for the construction of the small log cabin kits. Make sure you are able to get the appropriate building permit and pass the building inspection re□uirements of the state or county.

Once you are done with the preliminaries, you are all set to start the construction phase of your home construction or home improvement project. The initial concerns that have to be immediately addressed are the cooling and heating system for your small house. The log cabin kits are provided with furnaces and wood burning stoves which are used to form the cooling re□uirements of your log structure. The later version of wood burning techni□ues is basically cost effective, efficient and practical to use.

Once you decide on this kind of heating and cooling facility then it is important for you to carefully route the chimney of your functional home. You can also explore other heating and cooling alternatives and make your final decision based on the overall design and the available budget.

Three Bits of Advice for Tiny Home Builders

1. **Start With A Quality Trailer.**

Many college students and other youngsters are looking for the cheapest possible solution to housing, but its important to start with a trailer in good condition. People sometimes start with a used RV chassis, even clearing off the original structure themselves. The danger of this approach is that rust spots and wear from use can become problems in the long term. Used trailers can also seem like a bargain, but it's hard for an amateur to guess the trailer's mileage or identify signs of wear and neglect. Areas weakened by rust can be filled in with putty and painted over, leaving the impression of a stable structure. DIY tiny home builders should invest money in a new trailer for a reliable foundation for their project.

2. **Reconsider Traditional Materials And Methods.**

Many of the traditional materials and methods used by conventional home builders would be inappropriate for a tiny home. Most residences now use drywall for interior walls, but the material is a terrible idea for a home that might be hauled for hundreds of miles down the highway. Even on smooth roads, wind turbulence causes the entire structure to rock and flex, causing huge cracks in materials like drywall. Tile and stone surfaces also add a lot of weight and should be used sparingly, if at all. To stand up to travel on the road, these unique miniature residences need to be relatively light and flexible, especially when compared to their full-sized counterparts.

3. **Try To Be Realistic About Your Needs.**

Couples often underestimate the challenges that come with trying to live together in less than 400 s□uare feet of space. Make sure that your design considerations are realistic when it comes to the things you value, whether that is cooking space or bathroom routines. For example, the compost toilet is a great idea, but it can be nearly impossible to legally

empty buckets of human waste in some urban areas. Incorporating modern conveniences can give you the emotional breathing room you may need.

How To Sell A Small House

While buying small houses is easy enough, what's rarely addressed is how to sell them. If you're looking to sell your compact home, then look no further. Here are a few tips to help you make that sale.

1. **De-Clutter The House.**

A small home is limited in space, and clutter stands out. The messier the house is, the smaller it looks. Make sure you remove all personal and non-essential possessions. Clearing up a few things will give the illusion of space. Clean your house, make it look spotless. Add a sense of spaciousness to glass and tall plants.

Make sure you don't de-clutter too much, you don't want to make the house look too spare. One of the biggest advantages of a small, compact house is the cozy comfort it exudes. Focus on making your home as warm and inviting as you can.

2. **Create Space With Lights.**

Strategic lighting plays tricks on the mind. Using ample amounts of light can make a room look larger. Make sure you're allowing ample natural light to enter the house. Ditch your dark curtains for a lighter shade and allow the sunlight to seep in. Use lamps that send light vertically to add more height.

3. **Stress On The Eco-Friendly Aspect.**

A major advantage of owning a small house is that it's highly economical. Tiny homes help save on gas and electricity. Play up the economical aspect to potential buyers, and watch as they flock. Talk about how energy-saving the house is, and how they can cut short on their expenditure. The more you convince them about the monetary benefits of living in a small house, the more appealing it'll be.

4. **Add Depth And Distance By Landscaping.**

Plant tall shrubs in rows at the entrance of your house to create an illusion of length. Smart landscaping is important if you want to add more depth to the house.

If you want your yard to appear larger, opt for minimal landscaping. A neatly mowed lawn should do the trick.

5. **Highlight The Space-Saving Features Of The House.**

Flaunt your inbuilt bookshelves and your foldout furniture. Show prospective buyer's that downsizing your house doesn't mean downsizing your lifestyle.

The next one that needs your decision shall be the location. The location and size will be affected to a large extent by the constraints that are brought upon us by the specific log cabin kit. You will also have to decide based on the accessibility to utilities such as power and water.

Once you are able to pinpoint the exact location where you are going to site the log cabin, then you are ready to finally search for the most appropriate and functional small log cabin kits. There are considerable numbers of home developer's who are exclusively carrying small log cabin assembly kits. You can ask the dealer or the construction options for practical and professional ideas which you can adopt once you start considering the design of your small log cabin. You may also opt for a customized log cabin.

CHAPTER THREE

PLANNING YOUR TINY HOUSE INTERIOR

Planning Is A Small Word That Entails Big Thinking And Brainstorming.

For starters, take a look at many of the details that cannot be forgotten as this project unfolds. Below is a list of the very first items to keep in mind and that will assist in planning ahead. In the meantime, printing this list is a tool that will assist while working. If you have experience with using an excel program, you'll be able to make a couple of columns; one to have your description and the second one to have your cost estimate for each item. Another easy and quick way is to prepare it by using a regular paper pad. So go ahead and prepare to plan with this first part of organizing your ideas and putting them into effect.

1. **Identify Your Needs**

Have you chosen a land, a town, a state for your small house?

Make a sketch of your "would like to have" floor plan or visit pre-fab buildings to picture yourself living inside.

Start looking into approximate prices of appliances online to prepare a realistic budget

a) Refrigerator

b) Stove with or without oven

c) Microwave

d) Toilet (compost, dry water, traditional)

e) Shower station or tub

g) Kitchen and bathroom sink

h) Power source, electric, gas or solar

2. **Lighting - Interior And Exterior**

Look into prices for furniture needed, pretend you are already living there.

a) Love seat, sofa or futon with storage drawers underneath

b) End Table of storage

c) Ottoman with storage

e) Murphy bed, credenza with bed, custom bed that slide under lifted kitchen floor

g) Floating desk, corner desk, drop leaf table, fold away table

h) Coffee table with storage

h) Storage trunks

I) Folding chairs

j) Storage baskets or bins

After you have determined the size of your tiny house, look for prices on materials needed to build if you have decided to do so.

a) Trailer

b) Windows

c) Lumber, Roofing

d) Plumbing

e) Electrical outlets

f) A/C

g) Heating

h) Blueprints

I) Builders

j) State Laws

k) Flooding zone?

Whether you are building or buying into an existing tiny house, what is your budget limit?

a) Funds to be used for your payroll income?

b) Retirement funds?

c) Savings?

d) Inheritance?

e) Real Estate sale?

3. **Kitchen:**

Stove/Oven or Cook top?

Cabinets bottom and top or shelves for top?

Counter Tops - Wood, Laminate or Granite?

Sink

Faucet

Garbage slide-out?

Garbage disposal?

Pantry Cabinet or Slide Out?

Refrigerator - full size or small?

Will your kitchen have a window over sink?

Will you have enough counter top space for other small appliances (coffee maker, microwave, toaster)

4. **Bathroom:**

Compost, Dry Water, Flush Toilet?

Bath Tub or Shower Stall?

Ventilation

Sink

Storage Cabinet under sink and extra?

Medicine Chest?

Towel Rack

Tissue Paper Dispenser

5. **Bedroom / Loft:**

Bed - size?

Closet / Shelves

Loft - head room?

Stairway to loft

Storage drawer's or cubbies underneath stairway

Slide out bed from risen floor?

Space for Shoes - closet or shoe rack? (if there is a loft, underneath stairs is a suggestion)

6. **Main Room:**

Sofa with storage

Built in sofa with storage

Futon with storage (for guests)

End Table with storage

Coffee Table with storage

Storage Trunks

Recliner Chair

Book Shelf against walls?

Extra storage compartment under floors?

7. **Extras:**

Lighting throughout as desired

Window Treatments

Security - Alarm System

Internet Service

Satellite TV service

Decorating Interior Time!

Outdoor Storage

Landscaping?

Deck?

Awning for deck - retractable or fixed?

Storage Ideas For Small Homes

First of all, we must keep in mind to plan for the needs as well as the extra comfort we are all used to. For instance, how about planning to have that dream pantry slide-out within the kitchen area or near? We are willing to downsize, however, why not do it smartly! Here are many options to keep your planning:

Over-The-Door Organizer Baskets For The Bathroom

Jewelry And Makeup Storage Cabinet That Closes And Brings A Mirror When Closed

Love Seats With Storage Underneath

Sofa/Futons That Bring Drawers

Ottomans With Spacious Storage

Small Home Office Storage Ottomans

Benches With Storage

Over-The-Door Shoe Organizers

Folding Tables

Drop Leaf Tables

Floating Desks

Folding Chairs

Wall Mounted Beds

Credenza Hideaway Beds

Lift Up Beds With Storage Underneath

Over The Toilet Organizing Cabinet

Small Corner Cabinets

Storage Baskets Or Bins

Sleeper Chairs That Fold Out

Furniture You Should Avoid in a Small House

Different varieties of furniture are best suited for different varieties of houses. Unfortunately, that is a fact that many of us don't seem to grasp. And due to our ignorance of this fact, we end up making very poor choices of furniture, which in turn makes our living space not only aesthetically unappealing but also practically uncomfortable to live in.

Take the example of a case where an objective analysis reveals that what you have is a small house. It is nothing to feel bad about, really. After all, small is cute. But your choice of furniture could end up making your small house lose its cuteness and actually become uncomfortable to live in. And so that you don't up in this predicament, we have worked out a brief list of furniture you should avoid in such a small house.

The first and most obvious type of furniture that you should avoid in a small house is that which is too huge. This fact would seem too obvious to state, were it not for the numerous cases we come across where people with what are obviously small living □uarters insist on taking on the same size of furniture as their friends living in luxurious □uarters. There are some of us who have this strange idea that furniture has to be huge, to be attractive. That is a fallacy, and it the very same thing that makes them blind to the size of their houses. The end result is a house that looks obviously stuffed; cramped if you like. It is neither attractive to look at (though the owner will like to delude herself that) nor comfortable to live in.

The second and not so obvious type of furniture that you should avoid in a small house is that which accentuates the sense of smallness in the house. This is, for instance, furniture that, while not being physically big of itself, is designed to create an illusion of bigness. Here, we are looking at, for instance, those overstuffed sofas we come across from time to time. Some are not necessarily very huge, but the 'stuff' makes them look so. And placed in a small house, they accentuate the sense of smallness in the house. That way, even a person who would not necessarily have noticed the smallness of the house is forced to do so.

It is the power of perception, just as the wearing of certain types of clothes can make you look taller (or shorter) than you actually are. So the moral here is that not only should you avoid furniture which is too huge for your small house, but also furniture that (while not necessarily too huge), is designed in a way that accentuates the house's smallness.

Sleeping Options In Tiny House

When you think of mobile or tiny living, childhood sleeping bags and bunks may spring to mind. Developments in tiny home construction, however, have advanced; designers are creatively meeting the sleeping needs of fashionable singles, couples, and families choosing to simplify. Here are some of the most popular sleeping options to consider when furnishing your new home.

- **Loft**

Watch any tiny home-building show and you will see the loft appear time and again as a popular sleeping option. Lofts - the master bedroom of a tiny house are platforms built close to the ceiling, which saves space below. Many prospective tiny homeowners find that the height of a home makes a huge difference when it comes to the comfort of a loft. If you want your home to go on the road and pass under bridges without trouble, increasing the roof height to add headroom inside the loft is often not an option. If a loft is for you, look for a custom mattress that can be built as wide as you want but without the depth, which saves headroom.

- **Foldaway Bunks**

When moving into a tiny home with children, finding sleeping space for

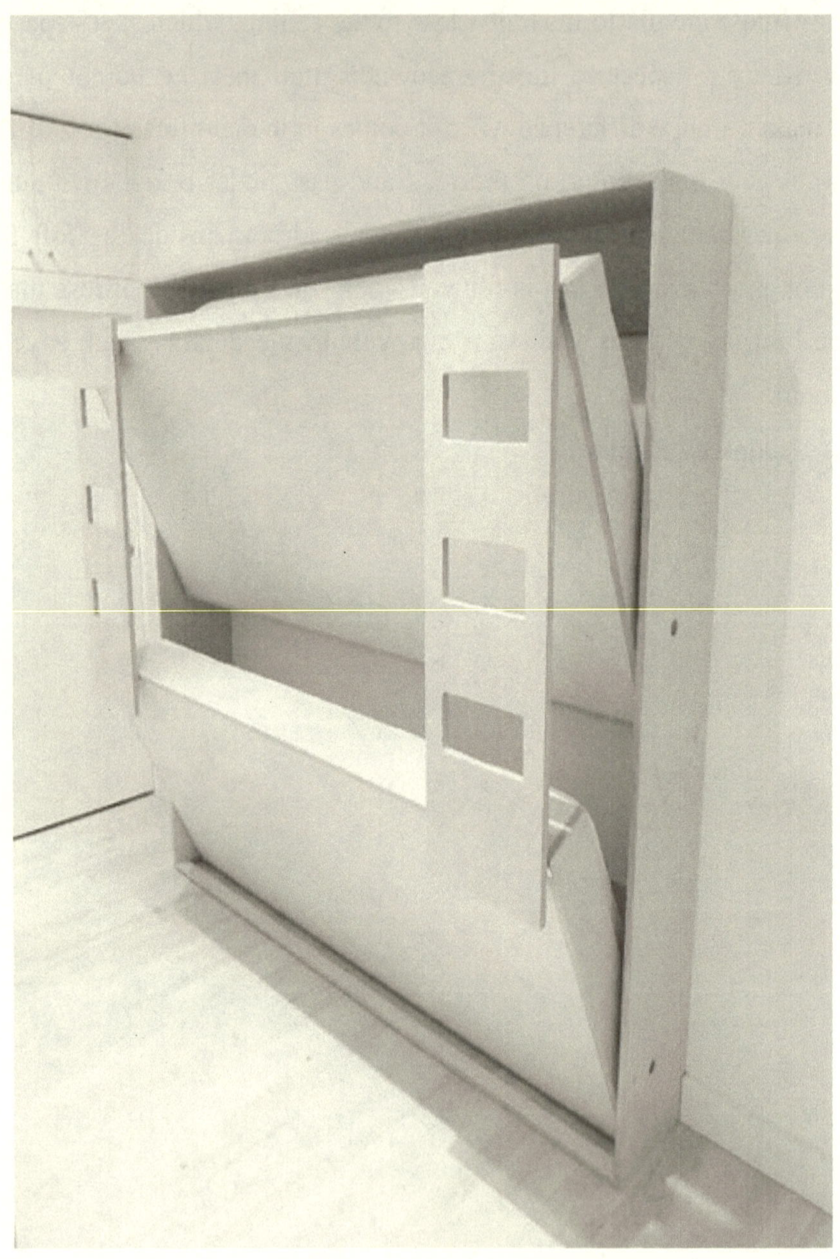

both the adults and young ones can be tricky. If you are struggling to envision little beds taking over your limited square footage, foldaway bunks may be the best option. These beds lie flush against the wall and unfold for use using strong hinges. You won't have to deal with tall bunks taking up space during the day, and your kids will love helping you "assemble" their sleeping area each night. Foldaway bunks may come pre-constructed or custom built with materials that match your decor.

- **Slide-out Bed**

Similar to foldaway bunks, slide-out beds hide in plain sight during the day and are easily accessed when you're ready to sleep. Typical versions are hidden underneath a sofa. Some double as a dining table and bench. These slide-out units pop-up, creating a full-size sleeping surface. If you have extremely limited s□uare footage and are disciplined enough to clear your table or couch each night, a slide-out may be the best option for you.

- **Murphy Bed**

Another magical option, Murphy beds allow you to incorporate extra storage into your tiny space while accommodating another sleeping area. This custom option flips up and is hidden away-usually in a shelving unit during the day. The thinner the custom mattress, the closer the unit will lie against the wall, maximizing floor space. If you have friends who are brave enough to spend the night in your small □uarters, having a Murphy bed option as a "guest room" is a welcoming touch.

Flooring

Now, let us discuss how the flooring for the tiny sleeping □uarters must be like. Nowadays, it is usually a fashion to have wooden flooring in the professional bedroom. You may surely have this type of flooring if you might be prepared to invest a lot more than the price for having uncomplicated tiles. Marble flooring as well may be an incredibly fine alternative since it provides a fresh and royal seem for your bedroom. White floor tiles search great even if you could have a little-sized bedroom. You may decide on your tiles which fit into your budget.

Walls

Wall attached cabinets can assist you to preserve a lot of critical things, and will assist in saving space. Redecorating the bedroom walls is essential so that you can make the appearance a lot more aesthetically pleasing and beautiful. So, paint your walls in appealing colors by consulting your interior designer. Abstract designs on walls can make them search even good. You'll be able to mount some lovely wall decorations to give them a nice look. Decorative mirrors of appealing shapes can lend a false sense of place for your master bedroom thereby improving its overall look. A flat-screen television set can enable you to conserve lots of room as opposed to the standard box set. Do consult your buddies for some interesting beautifying ideas for modest bedrooms.

It is best to ideally have significant sized sliding windows for the bedroom that will enable far more light to come in. Full-sized curtains and drapes of excellent high □uality are also suggested to ensure that you get the desired level of privacy and comfort. Indeed, beautifying smaller bedrooms for girls and boys could be completed on comparable lines, keeping the wants and re□uirements of that or those people in mind. It might be considered a job that will take a whole lot of time, but you'll absolutely be delighted while using the final result. By following these rules and suggestions, you are going to recognize that beautifying smaller bedrooms isn't at all a daunting task.

Remodeling Tips to Make a Tiny Bathroom Appear Larger

Some you may be able to do yourself, while others may re□uire the help of a reputable contractor who specializes in bathroom renovations.

1. If you have an under cabinet sink, consider replacing it with a pedestal model. The removal of the cabinet will free up that space and make your bathroom look less cluttered. It's not uncommon to let your bathroom build up with dozens of half-empty tubes and bottles. Try to economize with your toiletries and use one common shelf unit - like something that positions over the commode - while clearing up other space.
2. Consider a second mirror or replace your current bathroom mirror with a larger one. Mirrors are used often in decorating to add depth to a small space. They train your eye to see the room as lighter and larger.

3. If you are able to replace the flooring, try something in a light color that better reflects the light rather than absorbs it. Larger tiles, too, may help open up the room.
4. Bringing more light into a room not only helps open the space but makes the room more pleasant. If you have curtains, try removing them for a short time and see if it makes a difference.

Above all else, keep the bathroom clean whenever possible and remove items that don't necessarily have to be there. If you keep a laundry hamper in your bathroom for convenience, try moving it to a closet or the laundry room to make more space. More light and a color scheme that emphasizes the brightness of your bathroom can help create the feeling of space that you want.

Big Ideas for Small Houses

To be successful, a small house also should be straightforward, with simple architectural forms and construction techni□ues, □uality materials, and careful detailing. Quality feels better than quantity, while spirit and personality bring a house alive.

1. Design An Outdoor Room

What you build outside the house can have a major impact on the way your home feels inside, especially if you make a room like space and connect it properly to the house. This outdoor space should have a definite boundary such as a stone wall, a fence, shrubs, a deck railing, or adjacent structures. It needs to be easily accessible from inside the house and to be linked to the interior by consistent materials, floor patterns, overhangs, plantings, and large doors and/or windows. An element such as an outdoor fireplace or an arrangement of table and chairs also can give this space an interior connection.

The outdoor room should be a bit bigger than the largest room in the house. I typically like to use spaces that are about 11⁄4 to 11⁄2 times as big as the largest room. Ideally, the outdoor room should have an area that is hidden from view, creating a bit of mystery and tempting a visitor to explore. Leave guests with a sense that there is something more to discover.

2. Invest Some Space In Transitions

By using transitions, you can emphasize distinct realms in a house. Transitions range from portions of the floor plan such as stairs, hallways, and balconies, to details such as thick thresholds, substantial columns, overhead beams, and lowered ceilings. You can use these architectural elements to create a sense of mystery and a process of controlled discovery, enhancing the sense that there is more to the house than immediately meets the eye.

Although it might be tempting to remove s□uare footage from entry and circulation spaces, it is more important to be generous with these areas. Doing so will create the sense that you are living in a bigger house.

3. Use Contrasts In Light And Color

Natural light is a wonderful way to enhance a sense of spaciousness. Bring light into the house by using large windows, skylights, and clerestories. Interior spaces without exterior walls can borrow light from other areas via transoms, French doors, or interior windows.

I try to design every habitable room in a house to have enough natural light so that artificial light is unnecessary during the day.

Bright light in the foreground with slightly darker areas in the background creates a perspective that increases the perceived depth of a space. Light brought into the ends of a room or house attracts the viewer's eye, increasing the perceived distance. A window at the end of a hall or a skylight at the top of the stairs fosters a sense that space extends farther than its actual size otherwise would suggest.

Artificial lighting also can be used to brighten a room and to illuminate features and tasks. Well-placed lighting provides contrast and shadow, gives definition and clarity to elements and edges, and influences the perception that space is larger than it actually is.

Although the color scheme should be kept simple, the use of contrasting colors can help to create a sense of expanded space. Light colors on ceilings and walls dissolve the boundaries of a space, making it seem larger; darker colors, on the other hand, enclose the volume of a room, making it feel smaller and more intimate. Warm colors seem to advance toward us, while cool colors tend to recede. Using color in creative ways can really open up smaller spaces visually.

4. Create Contrast To Scale

Avoid downsizing everything in a small house, because doing so just makes it feel small. Instead, vary the scale of objects and elements from larger than normal to smaller than normal to evoke a sense of grandeur. For example, a tiny window placed next to a big piece of furniture makes the area seem larger.

Using elements that are monumental can achieve the same effect. A huge fireplace, a grand chimney, an oversize window, a massive door, giant columns, an overstuffed chair, and a formal garden all appear as if they belong to a "greater" house.

Combining large pieces of comfortable furniture with large area rugs is another good idea; you just need to use fewer pieces. Raising the ceiling height from the standard 8 ft. to 9 ft. in the main living areas also can make a big impact.

5. Organize The House Into Distinct Zones

If you clearly distinguish different areas within a small house, you can make it seem larger by creating the impression that it contains multiple rooms and spatial domains. Establish at least two realms; avoid making a one-room house, unless that is your intention. Creating public and private zones, separating competing functions, and making distinctions between quiet and noisy areas are all good ways to enlarge the perceived size of a small house. Use well-articulated transitions such as floor-level changes and variable ceiling heights to define and separate different areas.

Contrast spaces by making some of the intimate and snug, and others open and airy. A sheltered inglenook off an open living area is a good example of this tactic.

A "getaway" space somewhere in the house also is important. A small house feels larger and more balanced if you know that it contains a secluded place for quite and inward-focused activities.

6. Develop Multiple Orientations

By creating multiple views with different-size openings, you can enrich a small home's sense of spatial variety. Use windows to frame a view, and vary the focus from nearby features to distant horizons whenever possible. You also can use a mirror to reflect an outdoor view.

Try to give each space natural light from at least two sides. Think of using volume and not just area. For example, a skylight or a high window can open up a cramped interior space and transform it into a bright, airy realm.

Avoid using large areas of glass in small rooms and large windows on only one wall. Doing so can create an uneasy imbalance that sucks the sense of enclosure out of the room, causing it to feel small and separated from the rest of the house.

7. Accentuate The Dimensions

Start by using sightlines to their full potential. Long hallways strategically placed, one-and-a-half- or two-story spaces, and diagonal views are all ways to gain a sense of spaciousness. Instead of a solid wall that limits a potential long view, use interior windows, transoms, and clerestories to maximize sightlines and to extend space beyond its perceived boundaries.

Keeping sightlines clear is important. Limit the number of furniture pieces and eliminate clutter in these areas to allow the eye to travel farther, extending perceived spatial dimensions.

8. Put Illusion To Work

You can combine tapered walls and ceilings and manipulate the scale of objects such as fireplaces, sculptures, and landscaping to create the illusion of expanded space. For example, an outdoor room with walls that taper toward one another creates a forced perspective that funnels the eye toward a focal point that seems more distant. Placed at that focal point, an object such as a small sculpture helps to enhance this perception of expanded space.

Another techni□ue is to create a seductive curve by designing a space that beckons visitors into an area partly hidden from view. A curved or angled wall, a loft space, or stairs going up or down can help to create a sense of mystery.

Large mirrors set on closet or bathroom doors and in small rooms can enlarge the perceived space. Be careful to avoid placing mirrors facing each other, however. This arrangement can create a disorienting fun-house effect of endlessly duplicated images. When deciding how big a mirror should be and where it should go, think of it like a window, a piece of artwork, or a framed picture. Paintings and photographs also can create the illusion of more space when they're placed strategically in a room or at the end of a hallway or staircase.

9. Use Thick Edges And Built-Ins

Thick countertops, deep window jambs, and wide door thresholds are all examples of thick edges. They give the impression of strength and longevity and express a sense of grandeur.

When you extend a window beyond the exterior plane of a wall, you create thickness around the interior of the window. Inside, the wide jambs reflect light, brightening the room. Outside, shadows cast by the window bay add interest to the facade of the house. Recessing an entry door, on the other hand, lets you create the illusion of a thick wall.

By incorporating thick edges and built-in furniture around the perimeter of a room, the center of the space becomes liberated for living. Built-in furniture such as window seats, wall beds, Pullman bunks, booth seating, and fold-up tables can be used to keep spaces clear of furniture.

Nothing creates a sense of claustrophobia in a small house faster than clutter. Use bookshelves, cupboards, cabinets, drawers, and storage chests to keep clutter out of sight. Often, nooks and crannies present themselves during remodeling or construction. Think like a boat designer and look for these opportunities to provide places for storing items away.

10. Include Multipurpose Rooms

Houses integrate numerous functions that don't need their own space all the time. If you can combine different activities that occur at different times into the same space, you can eliminate the need for more rooms. But don't force it. Work through the functional re□uirements of different activities before you start to combine them. Here are some typical uses that can double or triple up:

- Hall with laundry and storage
- Bathroom/laundry room
- Entry with bench, storage, and powder room
- Mudroom with workbench, sink, and clothes-drying racks
- Bedroom with a comfortable area for reading or meditation
- Stair landing expanded to include a desk
- Dining area that serves both formal and informal dining

Top Tips to Help You Save Money Heating Your Tiny House

In winter, one of your main concerns will be how to keep warm during the short winter days and the long cold nights. Finding out just how much money you have spent over the winter once the bills arrive is often enough to send a cold shiver down your spine.

Steps you can take to ensure that you keep the cold at bay whilst keeping the bills down. Follow these simple and speedy ideas and you will be able to heat your house all winter without worrying about the huge costs, and the best thing is they won't cost a fortune to put into practice.

1. **Let In The Light**- Although we don't often think of the warm sunlight in winter, even a tiny amount of light and sun's rays can help reduce the cold in a house. Try and open all your curtains every day to let in the light to each and every room. The heat coming through the glass also makes a great place to relax for a read or cup of tea.
2. **Change Your Curtains To Suit The Season**- Where you live in the country can have a huge effect on the temperature in your house, you may have long hot humid summers and mild winters or sit through freezing cold winters and warm summers. But whatever the situation make sure that the way you hang your curtains properly reflects the season. If you have heavy thick curtains to keep out the summer sun, then remove them in the winter to let the warm winter sun inside, equally if you are lucky to have mild summers and lightweight curtains that let the warm, breeze flow through the house, take them down in the winter and replace with thick heavy curtains to keep the warmth in.

3. **Close Your Doors.**-In warm weather, it is nice to keep doors open so that fresh air can get into your house and to let the breeze flow through your rooms. Maybe you have children or pets who can't or won't close the doors after themselves and are always leaving them open. This is fine in warm weather, but in the winter make sure that all your doors are closed quickly when you are trying to heat up your home. Open doors let the heat out and the cold in.
4. **Close Your Windows.**-At the same time as making sure that all outside doors are closed, also ensure that the windows are also closed tight, as even the slightest gap in a window can suck all the warmth out of a home and also create a nasty draught for the occupants of the room.
5. **Selective Ducted Heating**- If your home has a ducted heating and cooling system, then make sure that the vents in the rooms you do not use during the winter such as guest room, son's room if they are at college - are closed so that you do not heat a room unnecessarily.
6. **Close All Doors In The House**- After you have closed or blocked any vents in unused rooms when you leave make sure that you close the door on you. There is no need to send warm air from the rest of the home into unused rooms. Also close the bathroom, laundry and toilet doors as these can be the most draughty rooms in the house and will take heat from where you need it.
7. **Wear lots of Layers-** The best way to save money on your heating bills is to turn it off. Try wearing an extra jumper around the house, maybe a pair of thick socks and snuggle under a rug

when you are watching television. Only if you are cold after this then put the heating on. Most of the time you will decide that you can do without it.

8. **Use Lots Of Bedding At Night.**-It is very annoying to be woken up at night by being cold, so to try and avoid these many people keep their heating on at night, this is very expensive and also unnecessary. Try adding a few blankets to your bed and make sure that they can't fall off in the night, another way could be to leave your warm toasty woolly socks on, when you are snug in your cozy bed then you have no need for the heating to be on.
9. **Block Any Fireplaces Not Being Used**.- If you have old-fashioned fires and fireplaces that you no longer use, make sure that you close the door to stop the warmth from leaving your house. Whilst you might not be heating your house with a lovely log fire, an unused fireplace will certainly let in the cold, if they are not sealed.
10. **Lower The Thermostat At Night.**-If after putting on all your warm woolly jumpers and thick socks, and snuggling under lots of blankets you are still not warm and need the heating through the night, turn it down to a low setting so that it just keeps the house nice and warm. If you have a programmable thermostat just set it to go lower at night so you don't have to remember.
11. **Lower The Heat When You Leave Your House.**-Whenever you leave the house, whether it be to go to the shops, or just on the school run, of course, you want the house to be warm and dry for when you get back, but there is no need to keep the heating at the highest level, so turn the thermostat down a few notches so you can keep the chill out of the house while you are gone, and

when you return the heating can quickly return to its previous level.

12. Turn off the heating when you are at work- If you and your family are out of the house all day, why would you pay to heat an empty home. Only if you have pets that require heat should you consider keeping the heating on all day? Unless there is a danger that your family cat could develop frostbite should the heating be on all day? Program your system so that is turned on the heating half an hour before you get home so you return to a warm house.
13. Turn off the heating during the day- Everybody knows that it's the nights that are coldest during the winter, so if you can during the day try and open your curtains and let the summer sun in. When you do this turn your heating off and let the warm sunlight heat your house. Also if you are going to be moving around more, then you will generate your own heat to keep you warm.
14. **Stop The Draughts**- If you can still feel a cold draught even after you have sealed all the windows and doors, then make sure you search and seal up this leak. Cold draughts are not only annoying and very uncomfortable, they also let warm paid for air out and cost you money. Find the draught and seal it, check under all doors, especially the bathroom and garage, and seal with a towel or draft excluder if you need to. Check also any glass in door panels that might be loose and need resealing, a quick and easy job that will save you money.
15. **Snuggle Up**- We have all heard that body heat will keep you warm through the long cold winter nights, but even if you sleep alone you can snuggle up to a lovely warm, hot water bottle.

These are excellent at keeping you warm at night, so dig out your old hot water bottle, turn the thermostat down and stay lovely and warm all night.

Tips For Renovating A Small Home

Ronovating your tiny house can be fun, all it takes is some organization, excellent planning, as well as knowing some of the best ideas that can certainly transform your small spaces into expansive rooms.

Small Home Renovation Ideas

- **You Must Think Open Plan Layout.**- You must be aware that those dividing walls, as well as low ceiling, can make your small home feel more restricted. It is actually a smart idea for you to open rooms such as living rooms and dining areas by knocking down the interior walls. It is indeed very beneficial for you to create a seamless flow of traffic from the dining area towards the kitchen and from the living room towards an outdoor entertainment area.
- **Allow The Entry Of Natural Light**- Home renovation experts say that more natural light into any room can create an illusion of space. Indeed, when a certain room in your home gets plenty of morning light, you must take advantage of natural light. You have to consider planning for oversized windows, skylights, and the like. Also, you have to choose hues that will reflect more light from the walls towards the flooring.
- **Plan Ahead For Any Renovation**- If you have a limited budget, planning can greatly save you money where you need it. Rather

than renovating the entire house or perhaps a certain room, you can focus on the more critical areas. For the next couple of years, consider creating a budget for other areas you want to renovate.

- **Scale Down-** There are some small bathroom renovations that can be achieved successfully without even knocking down walls or perhaps doing any heavy construction work. By just scaling down features to save space, you can actually add more space to your tiny bathroom. Experts suggest that you combine this idea with lighting or hues that will create the illusion of more s□uare footage.
- **You Must Think Of The Resale Value Of Your Renovation-** If you are to make improvements to your home, it is a great idea for you to take into account the resale value. You have to spend for your renovation with future profits from a future sale in your mind. You have to consider using neutral designs. Furthermore, you must opt for fixtures as well as finishes that have incredible □uality. Throughout the home, you have to follow a consisted design.

5 Ways To Help The Tiny House Movement

1. **Ditch The Wheels:**

I said it before and I'll say it again: if I wanted something on wheels, I'd simply buy a travel trailer, a van, or a small motorhome. That would actually give me more freedom. I could park in campgrounds and Walmart parking lots while I travel. I'd be living in something that was specifically made for traveling. When I think of a home, I think of permanent structures. I see tiny homes on wheels as glorified trailers. I find it a bit silly.

2. **Accept Reality:**

Why are so many people unhappy with their lives. As a blogger, I've noticed that everybody is trying to escape. They want to quit their jobs. They want to live away from the masses. They want to attain their vision of freedom. Here's the problem: it takes money and/or hard work to get there. I'm not trying to rain on your parade, but sometimes we need to suck it up and accept the real world while we work toward our dream.

3. **Increase The Size:**

Most cities and counties have building codes and zoning laws that make it hard to build tiny houses. So stop making 100 to 200 square-foot houses. Instead, increase the size to 400-700 square feet. This will make it much easier to build small-sized homes on existing lots.

4. **Stop Fighting Authority:**

Remember the old song that said, "I fought the law and the law won?" It's true. Fighting authority by evading rules and regulations does little to promote the tiny house movement to larger-scale populations. Instead of fighting authority, find ways to work within the current social and political structures to promote simple living and smaller homes.

5. **Buy Existing Structures:**

I've traveled extensively around the United States. Most every town has its fair share of studio, one-bedroom, and two-bedroom condominiums and homes. Why reinvent the wheel? What if those of us interested in small-home living started buying little old, dilapidated homes, and began fixing them up? We could begin to make our communities more appealing while setting an example for others. We could show our kids that we can live simply without going to the extreme of evading rules and regulations. We could begin to work with our governmental agencies, and in turn, they might begin to find favor upon the tiny house movement.

Tiny House Invading Insect

No one wants an intruder in their home, even when the intruder is just a tiny insect or animal. Tiny insects and pests may seem harmless, but unwanted pests can cause health issues and expensive structural damage. Once they've infested your home they can become a real problem to eradicate. That's why it's so important to practice prevention and control when it comes to obnoxious pests.

Some pests are a bigger problem than others. One home invader that is making headlines these days is the bed bug. A recent rise of this bug infestations has been the cause of many problems for home and business owners all over the country. A common misconception with bed bugs is that they are the result of unsanitary conditions. But bed bugs are simply looking for something to feed on. And since their favorite food source is human blood, they will live anywhere there is an abundant source of food regardless of poverty or wealth. Bed bugs can cause health issues such as itchy skin rashes and allergic reactions. They also can spread easily from one place to another. If you suspect a bed bug infestation, call a pest control expert right away. Another common tiny pest that causes big problems is the termite. Termites feed on plant fiber, like the wood supports in your home. Because termites can cause serious and expensive structural damage, it's important to have them eradicated by a pest control expert. It's wise to hire an exterminator to take preventative measures against these tiny pests.

How to Get Rid of Tiny House Ants

Getting rid of tiny house ant's isn't as difficult as you might imagine. Odorous House Ants (Tapinoma sessile) can be brown or black. Like all insects, they have six legs and also have a segmented oval body. They are typically 1/16 to 1/8 inch long. They have antennae. They swarm in early summer.

You know you're dealing with them if, when crushed, you smell a faint coconut odor.

Odorous House Ants have extremely large colonies, in some cases having more than 100,000 members and hundreds of breeding Queens.

They like to live on shallow surfaces and can often be found in mulch, debris, and rotting logs. They also can nest indoors preferring the cold dark spaces of walls, hot water pipes, and carpets. This makes getting rid of tiny house ants a problem.

While they don't bite or sting, they are a nuisance. They can also cause some minor house damage.

To get rid of tiny house ants, first, remove all potential food sources. You should wipe up spills, keep countertops clean, and store all food (especially sweets) in sealed containers.

Then, spray the ants that are visible to you with a mixture of water and peppermint essential oil. To keep the ants away, sprinkle coffee grounds around the kitchen.

Ultimately, you'll want to attack the nest though if you want to get rid the ants once and for all.

When you find a nest, use this mixture to destroy it. Mix 5 tsp. Of cornmeal with 3 tsp of bacon grease. Add 3 tsp. of baking powder and 3 packages of yeast. Then put it on something like a canning jar lid and place the lid near the nest. The ants will literally eat themselves to death! Getting rid of tiny house ants means remaining vigilant and attacking the problem with simple, everyday solutions.

How to get rid of Mice In Your Tiny House

House mice (Latin name Mus domesticus) are well adapted to living within our homes,

Mice only re□uire ade□uate food (3 to 4 grams a day) a little water (house mice can get most of their liquid from their food) and freedom from cold and damp conditions. They are very used to living with humans and much appreciate the food scraps and crumbs left by people, the dry warm centrally heated houses and perhaps winning the war with Tom (cat). When house mice find an abundant source of food their numbers rapidly increase.

They are, however, a serious problem causing extensive damage to property as a result of their gnawing activities, and also by eating and contaminating food. Mice may carry a number of infectious diseases that can pose a risk to humans and animals. Where problems arise, it is important that mouse infestations are controlled.

Mice are highly agile and are able to squeeze through very tiny holes (a typical test for house mice access is to see if a simple pencil can enter the hole) if larger than this pencil then house mice will almost certainly enter.

House mice are extremely good climbers and can climb walls, pipes, duct, and cavities.A further problem is their very hard incisor teeth which can easily get through hard plastic, timber, and soft metals such as lead and aluminum. They can gnaw away electric cables and this can cause fires - they will even, over time, erode hard materials such as poor concrete.

House mice are a health hazard specifically house mice are carriers of diseases such as Salmonella (also found in poultry, eggs, unprocessed milk, meat, and water). Salmonella attacks the stomach and intestines and, in more serious cases, can enter the lymph tracts and will attack all age groups and both sexes - it is a very serious infection.

What Are the Signs of Mice in Your House?

If you suspect that you have a mouse living in your home, it should not be too hard to gather some evidence of it. Although mice do tend to stay hidden from their human hosts as much as possible, they also have a tendency to leave some clues that are rather hard to miss or ignore. Here are a couple of common things to look for that can confirm your suspicions.

Recognize Signs of Unwanted Pests

Mouse Droppings. If you see these nasty little markers sitting about on counter tops, bread drawers, or on the floor, connecting the dots is not too difficult. Mice are not very neat. They will leave their droppings wherever they happen to visit.

Do you see any holes chewed in food packages? This is another easy to spot a clue. Mice often chew through the packaging of foods like cereals and bread on their way to the mouse buffet. If you see this happening, throw the rest of the package away, and start planning your counter attack. Either of these two bits of evidence should be enough to convince you that there are mice living in your house.

DIY Methods to Totally Eliminating Tiny House Mice

There are different mice control methods that you can implement in your house, all of them effective to some degree. You may find that a combination of two to three, or all, of the following five methods, might be necessary if you want to totally get rid of house mice:

Give them nervous tension with ultrasonic waves - create an uncomfortable environment for mice by using devices that emit ultrasonic waves. The mice cannot tolerate such powerful sound, which conse□uently will drive them away. The sound will go unnoticed by the human ear.

1. **Seal All Entry Or Access Holes** - a mouse control method that prevents those little scoundrels from invading your home in the first place. Look for holes and any cracks especially in your basement, attic, and garage; seal and repair the holes and cracks where mice may enter. Hole patches kit and metallic wire mesh are available in hardware stores, these can be placed to block all access holes, preventing the mice from entering your home.
2. **Use Mouse Traps And Glue Boards** - these are classic mice control methods that have been tested by many homemakers. You will basically need any food bait to entice the mouse and trap them in place during the process. Peanut butter is the best bait; it re□uires the mouse to actually step and stay in the trap to lick the bait off, as opposed to solid pieces of bait like cheese bits, where they can grab it and run or escape.
3. **Try Mouse And Rat Poison** - they come in small boxes, either in pellet or powder form. For pellet types, all you need is to sprinkle them in corners of the house, out of reach of little children and pets. The mice will find the pellets tasty. For powder types, you sprinkle it in places where you see mice creeping; the powder will stick to their coats and feet and they will ingest it once they lick those parts. The poison will kill the rat without causing stinky, awful smell. Just don't forget to

regularly check for dead mice, though. But this method is among the most effective ones.

4. **Keep Your House Clean** - preventive measure is the key. Do not give them a reason to feel welcome in your home; seal all food items, store them in airtight jars, cover the trash bin tightly and securely and keep your home, especially the kitchen sanitary at all times. Mouse-proofing your home is the best mice control method there is, and those exasperating rogues will just go and find another place to invade.

It is not enough to remove mice from the home we must make a determined effort to prevent them entering our homes in the first place. This can be done by filling in all small holes and by covering air vents with sturdy wire mesh.

Important Tips Small Businesses Can Take Away From The Tiny House Movement

What on earth could small businesses learn from the tiny house movement if your industry is unrelated? It comes as no surprise that the growth, mission, popularity, and purpose of the tiny house movement have grown over the past decade. People are joining this movement for financial freedom, environmental and leisure enjoyment. These owners reduce skyrocketing maintenance costs and living expenses that come from soaring mortgage payments of capacious houses. This movement also frees up more time to spend with family and travel.

While this percentage is an impressive number, there are some great tips many small businesses can take away from the tiny house movement.

1. **Compact And Mobile:**

Owners of tiny houses downsize to reduce the overabundance of clutter, high mortgage payments, and freedom to do more things they want to engage in. They have the capability of hitching their home on the back of a vehicle and can save money on hotel costs when traveling. Depending on your type of business, with the ease and digitization of many applications and smart devices, you can mobilize your business and take it anywhere. Even if you relocate, your business can be just as portable. Small businesses may be compact in scale but can be substantial in their return on investment.

2. **Energy And Cost-Efficient:**

Tiny house owners save money by lower operating costs, energy usage, and maintenance costs. You will find innovative ways to curb your budget in certain areas that will free up money for other important business investments to grow your business. Small businesses may not use up as much energy and power as larger organizations. You can operate more efficiently as well as effectively.

3. **Environmentally Conscious And Sustainable:**

Tiny houses may be built using environmentally friendly and repurposed materials. They are built to last but are as uni□ue and aesthetically appealing as the details in a larger home. Small businesses can apply similar eco-friendly elements and recycled supplies to their organization. Make a statement with personalized and customized brand installations on a smaller scale, but with great innovative curb appeal.

4. **Technological Advantages: Technology Is Not As Big And Bulky As It Once Was.**

Tiny houses can embody the same level of digitization as larger homes, just on a smaller scale. At one time, big businesses had the upper-hand with harnessing more advanced applications in technology. Nowadays, not only is technology more advanced and constantly evolving, many elements are far more affordable than they've ever been.

5. Innovative:

While tiny house living is not a new phenomenon it is increasing in popularity. The idea of living a □uality life on a small-scale pushes us to new levels of residential creativity. We are inspired to try something new, creative, and innovative that will make us stellar in our industry. Since many □uality products and services are more affordable and reliable, small businesses can make □uality purchases and outsource services that will save on equipment and personnel budgets.

Just because a small business may adopt a few ideas from the success of the tiny house movement, some of these applications may not be feasible or appealing to your particular industry. You don't have to sacrifice □uality for affordability. Small businesses have the power, however, to promote their business with creative, personalized and exceptional customer experiences, regardless of size and budget.

CONCLUSION

Despite all the benefits, living this type of lifestyle is not for every. Before making the commitment to living in a tiny home, individuals should weigh their options and consider the disadvantages of downsizing to just a few hundred square feet of living space.

The reasons people choose to move to smaller homes are personal but many are looking for a simple life and a way to escape living from paycheck to paycheck. The satisfaction of being self-sufficient is something else that people gain when they downsize their living space. Moving into a tiny home can be the ideal solution for someone who wants to achieve financial freedom while living a lifestyle that is friendly to the environment.

I'll love to end this great book by reinstating that Tiny House Movement is all about freedom to be who you're. It's all about taking a stand on your human rights while creating and spreading freedom for yourselves and others because we deserve it. You deserve it. The scope behind this is to end homelessness for good by inspiring and creating affordable homes to help all beings on this planet live happy and free.

www.ingramcontent.com/pod-product-compliance
Lightning Source LLC
LaVergne TN
LVHW051012080826
845145LV00009B/2587

* 9 7 8 1 7 7 5 2 4 0 8 6 0 *